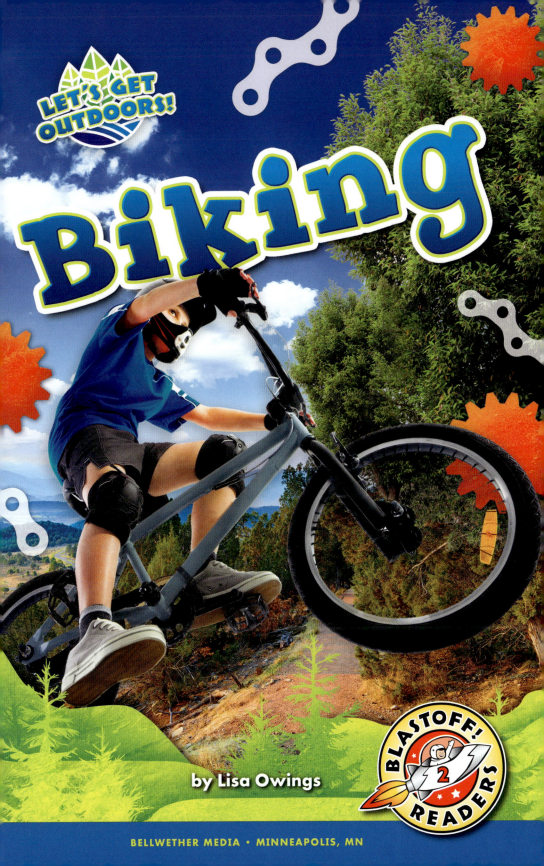

Blastoff! Readers are carefully developed by literacy experts to build reading stamina and move students toward fluency by combining standards-based content with developmentally appropriate text.

LEVELS

 Level 1 provides the most support through repetition of high-frequency words, light text, predictable sentence patterns, and strong visual support.

 Level 2 offers early readers a bit more challenge through varied sentences, increased text load, and text-supportive special features.

 Level 3 advances early-fluent readers toward fluency through increased text load, less reliance on photos, advancing concepts, longer sentences, and more complex special features.

★ **Blastoff! Universe**

Reading Level

 Grade K

 Grades 1–3

 Grade 4

This edition first published in 2023 by Bellwether Media, Inc.

No part of this publication may be reproduced in whole or in part without written permission of the publisher. For information regarding permission, write to Bellwether Media, Inc., Attention: Permissions Department, 6012 Blue Circle Drive, Minnetonka, MN 55343.

Library of Congress Cataloging-in-Publication Data

LC record for Biking available at: https://lccn.loc.gov/2022038743

Text copyright © 2023 by Bellwether Media, Inc. BLASTOFF! READERS and associated logos are trademarks and/or registered trademarks of Bellwether Media, Inc.

Editor: Rebecca Sabelko   Series Design: Andrea Schneider   Book Designer: Laura Sowers

Printed in the United States of America, North Mankato, MN.

Table of Contents

What Is Biking?	4
Parts of a Bike	8
Biking Gear	14
Biking Safety	18
Glossary	22
To Learn More	23
Index	24

What Is Biking?

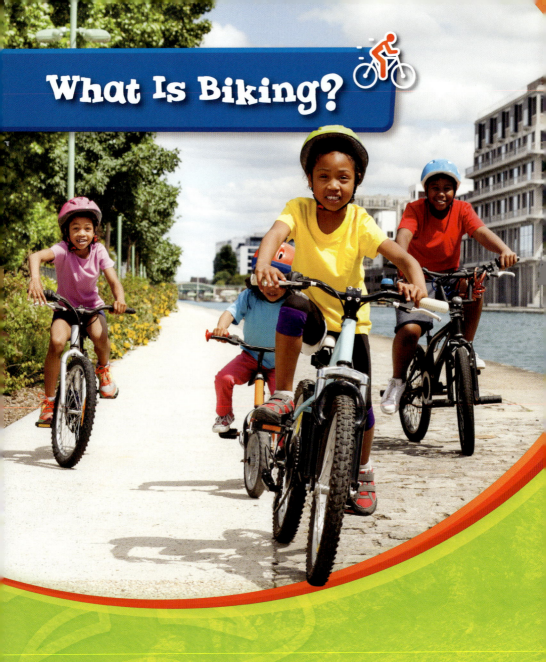

Biking is riding a bicycle. People around the world use bikes to get around.

Many people bike just for fun. Some enjoy racing or doing tricks.

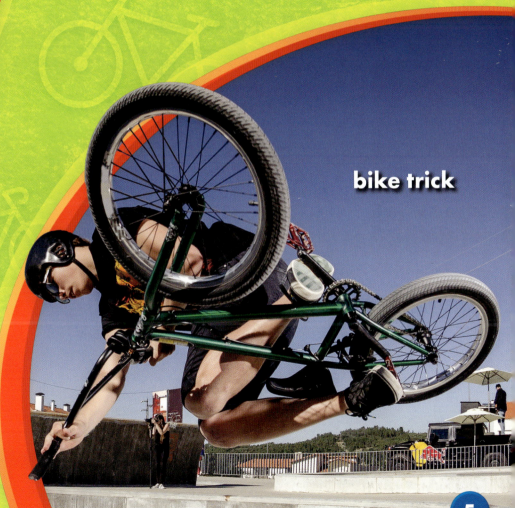

bike trick

Some bikers speed down roads or park paths. Others ride on forest trails.

Favorite Biking Spot

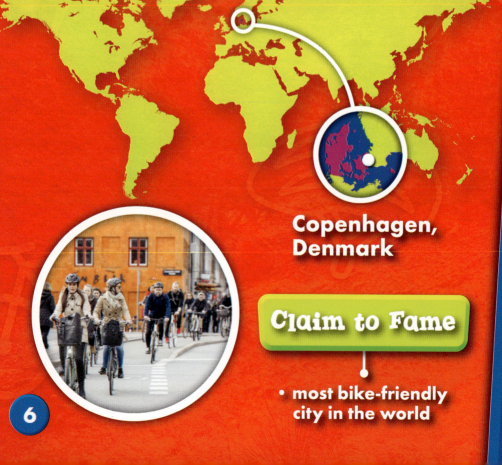

Copenhagen, Denmark

Claim to Fame

- most bike-friendly city in the world

forest trail

skate park

Bikers can learn tricks at skate parks. Biking can take people anywhere!

Parts of a Bike

People ride road, mountain, **BMX**, and **adaptive** bikes. All bikes have the same basic parts.

Bikers push **pedals**. The pedals turn a **chain**. It moves the back wheel.

pedal

chain

BMX bike

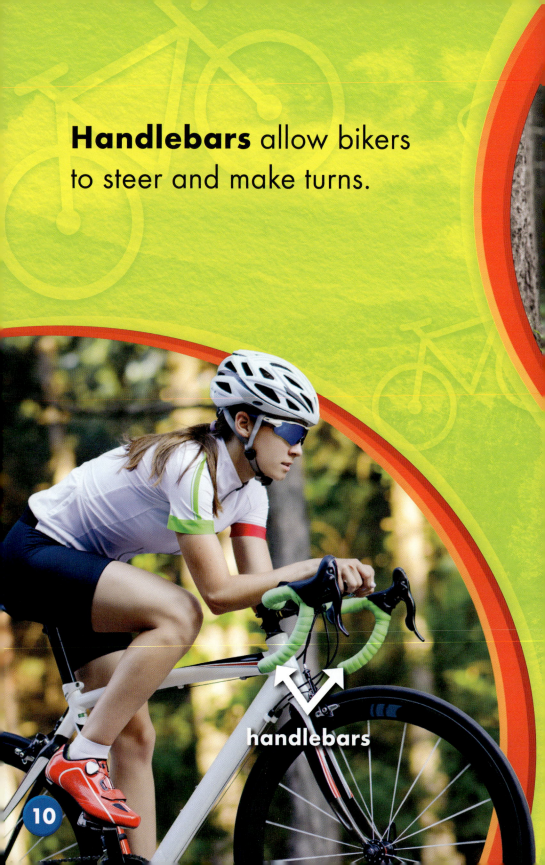

Handlebars allow bikers to steer and make turns.

handlebars

hand brake

Brakes stop bikes. Bikes can have hand or foot brakes. Hand brakes are on handlebars.

Shifters allow bikers to change **gears**. Some bikes have one gear. Others have many.

12

Lower gears help bikers pedal uphill. Higher gears let bikers travel quickly!

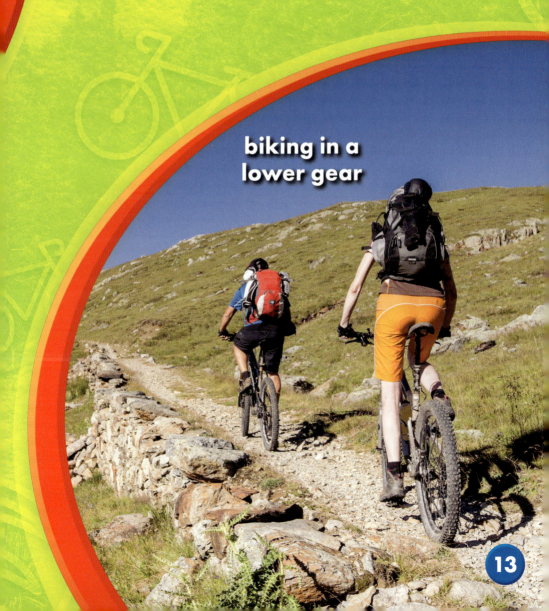

biking in a lower gear

Biking Gear

Water bottle holders help bikers store drinks. Bells let others know bikers are nearby.

Lights help others see bikers when it is dark.

light

Bikers must always wear a helmet to protect their head. Helmets must fit well to be safe.

Biking Gear
- helmet
- bell
- light
- water bottle holder

Bright clothing makes bikers easy to see.

Biking Safety

Bikers should check their bikes before riding. Flat tires or old brakes are dangerous.

Bikers must follow **traffic** rules. **Hand signals** help bikers avoid crashes.

Biking Hand Signals

left turn

right turn

stop

Bikers should look out for cars and other dangers. Bikers ride with friends to stay safe.

Buddies also make biking more fun!

Glossary

adaptive—made for people who have disabilities; a disability can affect how a person does some activities.

BMX—short for bicycle motocross; BMX is a racing sport with jumps and tricks.

chain—the part of a bike that connects the pedals to a wheel

gears—parts on bike wheels that can be moved to control speed

hand signals—movements of a biker's arms and hands to show they are about to turn or stop

handlebars—bars riders hold onto that control a bike's direction

pedals—the levers bikers push to power a bike; bikers pedal bikes to make them move forward.

shifters—levers usually on the handlebars of a bike that are used to change a bike's gears

traffic—related to the movement along a street

To Learn More

AT THE LIBRARY
Bassier, Emma. *Bike Safety*. Minneapolis, Minn.: Cody Koala, 2021.

Sommer, Nathan. *Bicycles*. Minneapolis, Minn.: Bellwether Media, 2022.

Yu, Dawu. *A Bicycle in Beijing*. New York, N.Y.: CCPPG, 2020.

ON THE WEB
FACTSURFER

Factsurfer.com gives you a safe, fun way to find more information.

1. Go to www.factsurfer.com.
2. Enter "biking" into the search box and click 🔍.
3. Select your book cover to see a list of related content.

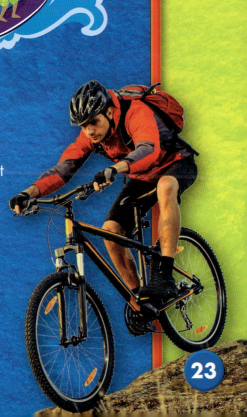

Index

bells, 14
bicycle, 4, 8, 9, 11, 12, 18
bikers, 6, 7, 8, 10, 12, 13, 14, 16, 17, 18, 19, 20
brakes, 11, 18
chain, 8, 9
clothing, 17
dangerous, 18, 20
favorite spot, 6
gear, 16
gears, 12, 13
hand signals, 19
handlebars, 10, 11
helmet, 16
lights, 14
paths, 6
pedals, 8, 9, 13
racing, 5

roads, 6
safety, 16, 18, 19, 20
shifters, 12
skate parks, 7
tires, 18
traffic, 19
trails, 6, 7
tricks, 5, 7
water bottle holders, 14, 15
wheel, 8

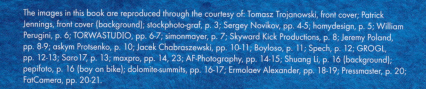

The images in this book are reproduced through the courtesy of: Tomasz Trojanowski, front cover; Patrick Jennings, front cover (background); stockphoto-graf, p. 3; Sergey Novikov, pp. 4-5; homydesign, p. 5; William Perugini, p. 6; TORWASTUDIO, pp. 6-7; simonmayer, p. 7; Skyward Kick Productions, p. 8; Jeremy Poland, pp. 8-9; askym Protsenko, p. 10; Jacek Chabraszewski, pp. 10-11; Boyloso, p. 11; Spech, p. 12; GROGL, pp. 12-13; Saro17, p. 13; maxpro, pp. 14, 23; AF-Photography, pp. 14-15; Shuang Li, p. 16 (background); pepifoto, p. 16 (boy on bike); dolomite-summits, pp. 16-17; Ermolaev Alexander, pp. 18-19; Pressmaster, p. 20; FatCamera, pp. 20-21.